To Walter
With love from
Margaret + Y

Whitburn
in old picture postcards

by William F. Hendrie

European Library ZALTBOMMEL/THE NETHERLANDS

Cover picture:
Composite postcard, 'Best of Luck From Whitburn.'

About the author

William F. Hendrie graduated from the University of Edinburgh in 1962 and began a teaching career at the Lindsay Technical High School. At that time many Whitburn pupils attended the Bathgate school for their secondary education and it was while teaching them history that he became interested in explaining to them the important role which their home town had played in Scotland's industrial past. His innovative work in teaching local history led to his involvement with the Scottish Television series 'History At Hand' and 'History In Store' and he was also invited to lecture on West Lothian by the Extra Mural Departments at Edinburgh University and Stirling University and to conduct field study courses in the district.

As well as being well-known to his former pupils, he is also known to many Whitburn families as the Headmaster of the West Lothian Education Authority summer camps from 1971 to 1996, which were attended by several thousand pupils from Croftmalloch, Polkemmet, Whitedale and St. Joseph's Primary Schools, whose interest in Scottish history he helped increase with project outings at Dounans Outdoor Centre, Aberfoyle, Belmont Outdoor Centre, Meigle and Middleton Outdoor Education Centre, Gorebridge.

Other books in this series by William F. Hendrie: Armadale in old picture postcards, Bathgate, Bo'ness vol. 1, Bo'ness vol. 2, Broxburn and Uphall, The Calders, Grangemouth, Livingston and Queensferry.

Acknowledgements

My thanks to Local Studies Librarian Sybil Cavanagh at West Lothian Library Headquarters and to Douglas McIndoe for allowing me to riffle their collections of postcards and photographs to select the pictures for this book. I am also grateful to Mrs. McIndoe and her sister Mrs. Helen Kirby for permission to reproduce photographs and for information and to Mrs. Mary Donnelly, Mrs. Anne Farrow, Mrs. Chrissie Prentice and Eddie Hughes for sharing their memories of Whitburn with me. The information about the postal system has been supplied by Mr. William Cochrane of Kanata, Ontario, Canada.

GB ISBN 90 288 1423 x

© 1999 European Library – Zaltbommel/The Netherlands

Introduction

Whitburn is situated in the heart of central Scotland, approximately midway between Edinburgh and Glasgow. Until Lord Wheatley's re-organisation of local government a quarter of a century ago in 1975 robbed it of its status, it was one of the county of West Lothian's six burghs. Now following the subsequent reform of local government in 1995 its affairs are administered by West Lothian Unitary Authority, but the inhabitants of Whitburn still take a strong local pride in their town's individual identity and keep alive the sense of community spirit, which has been its hallmark for well over 200 years. Whitburn takes its name from its situation on the banks of the little White Burn, a reminder of how clear and pure the waters of the Almond, which forms the town's northern boundary, were in years gone by. It first became an independent parish in 1713, when it was separated from Livingston. Religious worship had been conducted at Whitburn since 1628 and the famous Covenanting leader, Donald Cargill is said to have preached there, but the first place of worship was not opened until October 1718. The first resident minister was Rev. Alexander Wardrope, who was licensed to preach around the year 1722. At this time Whitburn was a small village, where most of its inhabitants depended on textiles for their living. There was a small cotton mill, but most of the inhabitants worked in their own homes as weavers. Whitburn first came to prominence in the 1760s when the new

southern toll road between Glasgow and Edinburgh was constructed through the parish and brought stage coach traffic. At Whitburn Cross the new road was crossed by the traditional route followed by the salters and carters from Bo'ness in the north as they travelled south to sell their products in Lanark and other places to the south. As the coaches had to stop at Whitburn Cross to pay their dues, it was natural for the travellers to seize the opportunity to enjoy a quick refreshment on their long, often cold and wet, 12-hour journey between the two cities. At first the toll keeper also sold ale and spirits, but soon inns and pubs clustered round the Cross to serve this trade as they still do today. The fastest of the coaches on the inter city route through Whitburn was known as 'The Flyer' and it is easy to imagine the hustle and bustle as it halted at the Cross as its first-class passengers, who travelled in comparative comfort inside and the second-class travellers, who huddled, crowded together exposed to the elements on bench seats on the roof, clambered down and clamoured to be served food and drink, during the brief stop, before it sped on again to keep up to time on its long journey to Edinburgh or Glasgow. The Halfway House, whose site was originally part of the Polkemmet Estate, is another reminder of the prosperous stage coach business, as it was built as a place to change the teams of horses to maintain maximum speed on the 44-mile journey. Polkemmet was for over 300 years the home of the Baillie family, the best known landowners in the Whitburn area. They came originally from Lanarkshire and bought their Whitburn property from Mr. Andrew Shaw in the year 1620. In the Baillie family, Thomas was the favoured name for the eldest son and the first six Lairds of Polkemmet all bore it. In the 18th century the sixth heir went into law and was appointed a Writer to the Signet in 1732. His successor, William, also followed a legal career gaining even greater distinction and wealth. He became one of Scotland's Law Lords at the Court of Session in Edinburgh in 1793 with the title of Lord Polkemmet. The Baillies climbed even higher up the ladder of Scottish society, when in the year 1823 son William was made a Baronet. During the next 100 or so years the Baillies followed political and military careers funded by their Whitburn estate and especially by the profits which they received from the coal mined beneath it. The old stone mausoleum where some of the family lie buried can still be seen at Polkemmet, which is now a very popular country park, but sadly the magnificent stately mansion was demolished during the early 1960s by its then owners the National Coal Board. The Whitburn area has always been rich in stone, ores and minerals, the Second Statistical Account of Scotland published in April 1843 noting: 'Several quarries are open in this parish. Whinstone is to be found. There are some good sand quarries, one of a white siliceous nature, which makes excellent garden walls. There is another of red sandstone. The most valuable mineral which this parish contains, is what is called the Crofthead or slaty black band ironstone of which a very fine field has lately been discovered lying between Fauldhouse beyond the village of Longridge. The change which this discovery has made upon this district is very remarkable. What was until the last century a solitary Moreland scene, has now become one of enterprise and industry. Tall chimneys are seen in all directions and clouds of smoke show the extensive nature of the operations which are carried on.' By the time of the Statistical Report coal was also being mined in Whitburn Parish at Greenrigg Colliery. Throughout the following century coal mining continued to grow in importance until a 100 years later in the 1940s Polkemmet Colliery was the largest employer in the area. By the late 1980s its closure and the total disappearance of the coal mining industry was a severe set back for Whitburn, but now at the Millennium the town is recovering and enjoying a prosperous new lease of life as an attractive commuter centre, from which the excellent road network makes it easy for workers to travel to jobs in Edinburgh, Glasgow and other surrounding places. While many of its new inhabitants find work away from the town they and their families are pumping new life blood into the local economy and their interest is helping to keep alive Whitburn's traditions and customs from its spectacular annual summer children's Gala Day to its nationally famous brass band. With its well-established churches and its excellent local schools, Whitburn is indeed proving a popular place to live and its population of only 5,232 in 1951 has now risen to over 12,000. It is hoped that the old views of Whitburn in this book will bring back memories to the town's older inhabitants and increase interest among newcomers in their home area's interesting past.

1 This picture postcard view of Whitburn Cross and East Main Street was posted in 1914, the year of the outbreak of the First World War. It was printed and published locally by Archer the Stationer as part of the Caledonia Series. Although the scene looks very different from the busy thoroughfare nowadays, with the laddie with the bicycle in the middle of the road the only piece of traffic in the entire street, the attractive historic clock tower of Whitburn's former Burgh Chambers, the Baillie Institute, is still a distinctive and familiar landmark. Whitburn's first Provost, Robert Gardiner, was elected in 1862 and continued in office until 1882.

The previous year the census showed that Whitburn had a population of 1,200. Councillor Alex. Bell, the town's last Provost, held office from 1971 to 1975 and later went on to represent Whitburn on Lothian Regional Council in Edinburgh. By this time the 1981 census revealed that Whitburn had a population of 11,965.

East Main Street, Whitburn.

2 It was from the Burgh Chambers in East Main Street that all of the civic business of Whitburn was conducted. For over a century Whitburn had its own local council governed by its Provost, Bailies and Councillors from its inception as a Police Burgh in 1861 until the Town Council was abolished during the revision of Scottish local government in 1975. The town's coat of arms with its coach and four, depicted on this postcard, which recalls the days when the stages used to halt to pay their tolls at the Cross, used to grace all of the town's official correspondence. The wheat sheaf in the lower half of the shield is an interesting reminder that for hundreds of years the parish of Whitburn was principally an agricultural one and that it was not until later than most other places in West Lothian that Whitburn became industrialised. The wheat sheaf has also been adopted nowadays as the badge of Croftmalloch Primary School as a reminder to its pupils that it is built on the fields of the farm of that name. The two symbols in the upper half of the town shield are described as estoiles and are linked to the Baillie family, while the wavy lines represent the White Burn and the River Almond. The coat of arms, whose colours were blue and silver, were designed by a Whitburn native, George F. Shields.

3   In this postcard photograph of Whitburn Cross looking towards East Main Street, which was taken shortly after the end of the First World War, it is interesting to note the changes which have taken place since the scene shown in the first illustration. Street lighting has arrived and this combined with the increase in traffic has resulted in the finger sign post being relocated to a less prominent position against the stone wall of the corner sweetie shop. Most prominent amongst the vehicles is the single decker bus. The paper posters stuck to the rear windows read 'Bathgate', 'Whitburn', 'Fauldhouse', presumably indicating the route which it followed. Regular time-tabled local bus services expanded greatly during the opening years of the 1920s, linking Whitburn with Armadale and Bathgate with connections to Edinburgh and Glasgow.

East Main Street, Whitburn.

4 Annie Sangster was one of the first conductresses on service buses plying to and from Whitburn. Here she is seen in her navy blue uniform, complete with peaked cap and leather satchel for collecting the fares. In return she issued long thin cardboard tickets in which holes were punched to ensure that they could not be used over again on a future journey. The military look of Miss Sangster's uniform was not coincidental as it was the absence of local menfolk fighting in the army during the First World War, which led to women being allowed for the first time to occupy such posts. Until then Whitburn women who had jobs mostly worked in their own homes as weavers in the domestic textile industry. Weaving had been a prosperous home industry in Whitburn during the 18th and 19th century, but by the time this photograph was taken it was in marked decline.

5 Three young men with a bicycle paused on the corner on the right, while the photographer took this picture postcard view of West Main Street. Apart from a few other residents standing by the doors of their homes the street is completely deserted in marked contrast to the bustling traffic which occupies it nowadays. The mention of the lack of traffic is a reminder that it was not until 1921 that Whitburn acquired its first police station, which was simply one room in the Baillie Institute. The strength of the force in the town in those days was one sergeant and one constable. The town's first purpose-built police station consisted simply of a lean-to building added to the east end of the three police houses built in 1936 at 87 to 92, East Main Street. By then the police establishment in the town had been increased to four, but they had also to patrol Blackburn, Fauldhouse, Greenrigg, Longridge and Stoneyburn! The present police station, which occupies a corner site in West Main Street, was first occupied in May, 1979 and cost £160,000 to build. The opening ceremony was conducted on 11th July by ex-Provost Councillor Alex Bell and when it was opened the police establishment consisted of one inspector, two sergeants and seventeen constables.

West Main Street, Whitburn.

6 Half a century has past since the previous photograph was taken and this picture postcard view shows West Main Street looking somewhat more familiar in the early 1950s.

WEST MAIN STREET, WHITBURN.   D.6430.

7   Back in time again this postcard picture shows a single horse-drawn cart as the sole traffic in East Main Street looking to the west over the Cross towards West Main Street. While Whitburn still had little traffic at the beginning of the 20th century it had had a post office since 1786. The first recorded Whitburn Penny Post hand stamp is for September 1833 and it was used until Rowland Hill's Uniform Penny Post was introduced in 1840. From then on only the Royal Mail was permitted to deliver letters and The Shotts Iron Company was taken to court and fined for breaching the new postal regulations by enclosing its letters in parcels, which were brought to Whitburn by its own private messenger and put aboard the Edinburgh to Glasgow mail coach as it passed through the town.

Whitburn looking West.

8 The view looking the opposite direction was captured in this postcard view taken in the 1950s. The message on the back states that the arrow pointing to the second house on the right was where the sender was staying. It is interesting to wonder if during their holiday in the town this visitor sampled the delights of an ice cream from Di Resta's Crossroad's Café. The Di Restas are one of Whitburn's two Italian catering families, the others being the Bonis with whom they have inter married and indeed on one occasion even swapped cafés. Before either the Bonis or the Di Restas, however, Whitburn's first Italian ice cream shop and café owners were the Francchittis and it was they who introduced local people to the pleasures of cones, sliders and in these pre-politically correct times, single and double 'Blackmen', ice cream with either one or two chocolate enrobed nougat filled wafers. Simply delicious!

EAST MAIN STREET, WHITBURN.

9 Photographer J. McLeod from Fauldhouse took and published this picture postcard showing a very early view of East Main Street. Notice the little girl on the right, who stood by her garden gate and looked on curiously as he took this photo. His picture also shows clearly the pot-holed state of the unmetalled road surface over which the horse-drawn cart disappearing into the distance towards the Cross had just bumped its ponderous way.

EAST MAIN STREET, WHITBURN.

Photographed and Reproduced by J. M'Leod, Fauldhouse.

10 This very early picture postcard view looks from West Main Street over the Cross to East Main Street, where again the canopied clock tower dominates the scene. The canvas awning pulled down to protect the display in the draper's shop on the north-west corner of the Cross and the sun cast shadows in the foreground suggest that it was a fine summer day when this photograph was taken. It is interesting to note the very early bus standing on the far side of the Cross and once again, the still unmetalled condition of the road surface.

The Cross, Whitburn.

11   Farther along West Main Street on its north side opposite where the swimming pool is now situated, stood this picturesque thatched cottage. This part of the street was known as the Clachan. A clachan was an old Scottish word for a very small village or a hamlet of houses. The iron gutter below the steeply pitched thatched roof, which was provided to drain away water, is a reminder that when in Victorian times Whitburn had a weather station at Polkemmet House, which provided daily readings long before the days of weather forecasts, the town was recorded as the wettest place in West Lothian. There were six weather stations within the then boundaries of the county and taken over a twenty-year period the one at Polkemmet recorded an annual average rainfall of 44 inches compared with 40 inches at Bathgate, 35 inches at Linlithgow and only 27 inches on the coast at Bo'ness. 1903 was an especially wet year with the Polkemmet weather station indicating a total rainfall of just over 55 inches compared with under 29 inches the previous year. In 1911 Whitburn suffered a drought and there was great worry in the town that the water supply would run dry.

12 Like the women and bairns in the previous picture of Whitburn's Clachan, Mr. Mitchell, with his measuring tape draped around his shoulders, came to the door of his draper's shop, when the photographer took this picture. He is accompanied by Mr. John White, who was a well-known local poet. The shop window is full of samples of material from which local men could choose the fabric from which they wished their new suits to be cut. Getting a new suit required several visits to Mr. Mitchell's to be measured and fitted. With his neatly trimmed moustache, he himself looks immaculate in his three-piece suit, complete with white handkerchief neatly tucked into the top pocket of his jacket and his gold watch chain on view. In the back shop Mr. Mitchell had a large raised wooden platform on which he sat crossed legged while he carefully cut out the pattern of the suits, which were ordered. The flat surface of the wooden platform also proved ideal for him to press the finished suits with a large flat iron called a goose, before each customer came in for a final fitting.

13 The years have moved forward almost half a century to 1953, when these other Whitburn craftsmen were photographed setting type at Hamilton's Print Works in East Main Street. The posters advertise various dances to be held over the Christmas and New Year period at the community centre, welfare and public halls around West Lothian to popular local band the Meltones. Prices of admission ranged from one shilling and six pence, seven-and-a-half pence in modern currency to a pricey two shillings and six pence, half a crown in old money. The poster for Whitburn Welfare or the Big Hall, as it was usually known, will bring back many memories of Saturday night dances.

14 This picture postcard view of Polkemmet House well illustrates its size and impressive appearance. With its thick stone walls and grey slated roof and turret it was the spacious home for over three hundred years of the Baillie family. As by far the best known and wealthiest of the landowners in the Whitburn area, the Baillies in Victorian times exercised a paternalistic influence over the town and its inhabitants, from paying for the Baillie Institute to providing for a token rent the land for Whitburn Bowling Club, which Sir William officially opened on 25th June 1887, to mark the golden jubilee of Queen Victoria's ascent to the throne. They also annually opened the grounds of Polkemmet House for various local events including summer Sunday School outings. Best known of the more recent members of the family during the 20th century was the 6th Baronet, Sir Adrian, who was Deputy Lord Lieutenant for West Lothian and who represented the county as its Member of Parliament when he won the seat in 1931 by his surprise defeat of the well-known Socialist Emmanuel, 'Manny' Shinwell. 1931 must have been a memorable year for Sir Adrian, because it also marked his marriage to the daughter of Lord Queensborough. From then on he tended to stay more at his new wife's home at Leeds Castle in Kent and at her town house in London's Mayfair and Polkemmet House sadly began to deteriorate.

POLKEMMET HOUSE. WHITBURN.

15   During the First World War, Polkemmet House was turned into a convalescent home for wounded servicemen, who were cared for by members of the Red Cross. Throughout the Second World War from 1939 to 1945, the house was again requisitioned, this time to house child evacuees, while the estate was turned into an army camp, first for British troops and later for officers and men of the Free Polish Army. Towards the end of the war the house was used for a short time to house an overflow of young TB-patients from Bangour Hospital and then in 1945 became the Trefoil School for handicapped children. The very worthy pioneering effort promoted by the Guide Movement, whose distinctive three-leaf badge it adopted, was rewarded with a royal opening when on 25th September 1945 Her Royal Highness Princess Elizabeth, now Her Majesty The Queen, carried out one of the first public duties which she performed on her own. This picture postcard view shows some of the Trefoil School's young patients outside the front door of the house.

16   This view of Polkemmet House with the Boy Scouts to the fore may have been taken on the occasion of the royal opening of the Trefoil School or at a later event connected with the school, before it moved to its present premises at Gogarbank on the western outskirts of Edinburgh in 1951. Soon afterwards Polkemmet became the Scottish Police College, but the house was not large enough to accommodate all of the 150 recruits in each training course and some had to be housed as a result in temporary huts at Townhead Gardens. As a result of this continuing problem, the college moved in 1960 to Tulliallan Castle in Clackmannanshire. Polkemmet was soon afterwards demolished. The remaining stable block and steading are now used as headquarters for the country park and as club house for the public golf course in its grounds.

17 Her Majesty Queen Elizabeth paid a second visit to Whitburn ten years later in 1955, two years after her coronation. Here the Queen's representative in West Lothian, the Lord Lieutenant, is seen introducing Her Majesty to Lothian and Borders Police's well-known Chief Constable Willie Merrilees, famed amongst other things for having successfully arrested a German spy at Edinburgh's Waverley Station and for introducing Walt Disney to the story of Greyfriars Bobby, which the American producer later turned into a popular children's film.

18 On the same royal visit in 1955 Her Majesty Queen Elizabeth, who was accompanied by His Royal Highness Prince Philip, Duke of Edinburgh, is seen chatting with Provost William Griffith as she returned to her official royal car, which is flying the Royal Standard. In the background can be seen the well-known Whitburn Roadhouse, beside the A8 road, which was in those days, long before the construction of the M8, the main route between Edinburgh and Glasgow.

19 The popular Whitburn Roadhouse is seen in close up in this picture postcard view. Built in distinctly art nouveau style, when it opened in the 1930s, it was a great novelty as one of the first facilities built out in the countryside to serve a main highway, the new A8 road, long before modern motorway service centres were ever thought of. Although it has now been given a new name, The Strathalmond Hotel, and a conservatory has been added, the Road House still looks much the same as when it was first built.

20 Earlier in Whitburn's history, transport in the district was all horse drawn such as this trim pony trap, owned by local grocer Hugh Dewar. The wicker work basket in which Mr. Dewar transported fresh provisions to sell to housewives around the town and to deliver orders can be seen at the back of the two-wheeled trap.

21　By the time of the First World War, some of Whitburn's more progressive traders had invested in new fangled motor vans. This one with its round port hole side windows like the one in Mr. Jone's the Butcher's van in the popular television series 'Dad's Army', was owned by Mr. Wood, the baker. As most of the town's menfolk were away fighting in the trenches in Flanders, it was driven by Miss Maggie Kay, as she did her rounds of the town delivering freshly baked rolls every morning and loaves of bread and tea breads such as scones, pancakes and cookies and cream cakes later in the day, ready for afternoon teas and as a treat after high teas.

The van with its roof rack for extra supplies, had solid rubber tyres and paraffin lamps for headlights. Miss Kay has a leather money bag slung over her shoulder to carry her change, all ready to serve her customers, who must have found having a delivery girl quite revolutionary.

22 Sadly some of the young Whitburn men who went to fight for their country in the First World War against Germany between 1914 and 1918, never returned home. They are remembered by the stone war memorial with its lone soldier, which was erected in the Public Park.

War Memorial, Public Park, Whitburn.

23 Some of the Whitburn men who survived were confined to invalid carriages, like this tricycle, which was a familiar sight in the town when it was used by Alexander Sangster.

24 The Whitburn Miners Welfare Association provided this ambulance long before the coming of the National Health Service in 1948. The gentleman struggling to pull the car is believed to be 'Sunny' Bryce, but why was he hauling it along the road? The combination of the presence of the local ambulance and the broken down car suggests that there may have been an early road accident.

25 Coming more up to date, this ambulance served Whitburn in the late 1940s. The gentleman wearing the cap is Councillor Joseph O'Brien from Armadale and the ambulance often ran over the hill road between the two towns transporting patients to Tippethill Hospital.

26　The route to Tippethill Hospital lay north along Armadale Road. The long sweep of the road as it climbed the hill and the long low line of the hospital buildings on the ridge can be seen in the background of this picture postcard view.

Armadale Road, Whitburn.

27 Tippethill Hospital, seen in this postcard view posted in 1903, was deliberately built in an isolated position on the hilltop between Whitburn and Armadale as an isolation hospital for infectious diseases. Most of its patients were children suffering from scarlet fever or diphtheria or measles. Right up until the 1950s all of these highly infectious diseases could prove fatal and children were therefore taken into hospital and isolated from their families for as long as two months, while the local Sanitary Inspector or 'buggy man', as he was known in Whitburn, fumigated their homes. The touching little message written on the wrong side of this card was typical of many sent by Tippethill's child patients. Some of the nursing staff who looked after them during their long weeks of separation from their parents are seen in front of the entrance.

The buildings were typical in design to that used for many Scottish cottage hospitals in small towns all over the country. After catering originally mainly for young patients, Tippethill was later converted into a geriatric unit for the elderly.

The Hospital. Kissing from wee Tom ++++++×××× Armadale.

28 Many of the Whitburn men who did return from the First World War found work sinking the two shafts at Polkemmet Colliery. Polkemmet was actually situated just outside the burgh boundary of Whitburn in the county of West Lothian. The work of sinking the first shaft began in 1913 and Polkemmet was often known locally as the Dardenelles, possibly because it was being dug at the same time as that horrific retreat was taking place in Europe. The sinking of the shaft at Polkemmet was equally a battle, partly because of geological conditions and partly because of the lack of skilled manpower caused by so many men being away fighting in the army. While the digging of a second shaft was begun in 1916, both were soon abandoned, because while working as a coal miner was a reserved occupation, the job of sinking the shafts to reach the coal was not and a suitable work force could not be maintained during the years of the hostilities. Work began again at the end of November 1918, but it took another three years to reach the coal.

The first coal was not brought to the surface until 1922 and the faces were not properly developed until the end of 1923. Polkemmet was originally owned by William Dixon, Ltd. In the picture the workman in the middle of the front row with the white beard is John Johnston, who was the engine keeper. He is holding a wee kitten on his knee as is the man next to him. Notice how very young some of the boys in the picture were.

29 Although female labour underground in the pits was banned by Act of Parliament in the 19th century, the use of women workers on the surface continued well into the 20th century. This photograph taken in the early 1920s shows some of the pit head workers. They are believed to be (back row, left to right): Jenny Johnston, ? McComisky, Annie Mcfarlane, Tam Fisher who was probably the overseer, Jennie Stevenson and Jean Brodie. Front row: Agnes Prentice, ? Dickson, middle girl unknown, Nan Hastings and Marion Prentice.

30 This photograph of Whit-burn miners also includes two women pithead workers and two very young boys.

31 After the First World War there were many prolonged strikes in the coal industry during the 1920s as the miners fought with their employers over conditions and rates of pay. To feed their hungry families soup kitchens were often opened. This photograph shows the cook and her assistants at the soup kitchen at Greenrigg Colliery. One of the women holds a metal mincer in her hand, while the men posed with the potatoes, which they were busy peeling.

32   With hard manual work, low pay and many strikes the 1920s were difficult times for Whitburn families but they still managed to enjoy themselves with simple pleasures such as this gathering of friends and neighbours in Lea Street to celebrate the birthday of Auld George. Auld George was probably Geordie Stewart and others in the photograph of the festivities are belived to include Agnes Neally, James Stevenson, Alex Brownlee, Lizzie Brownlee, Tammy Miller, William McMorran, William Rennie, Peter McGowan, John Brown and Martha Wilson. Families were very large as compared with nowadays as can be seen from the horde of bairns crowded into the picture. This photograph is a splendid example of the community spirit which existed in Whitburn at this period and of how events such as this spanned all of the age groups from babies in arms to grandparents. The clothing worn by the children and other guests at this street party provides an unusually detailed glimpse of how local people dressed at this time.

33 Underground motive power in Polkemmet Colliery was much more modern than the patiently plodding pit ponies of earlier years. Miners at Polkemmet were transported to and from the coal face on what were described as 'man riding trains'. These could carry around one hundred miners at a time. This rare picture of conditions underground shows two of these trains, the one on the left empty after having delivered its load of miners to the face and the other one on the right crowded with men about to begin their eight-hour shift. The brakeman can be seen with his hand on the emergency brake to the right of the red rear warning light. This high-roofed main underground road from the foot of the two 1,400 foot shafts to the coal face, was lit with electricity produced by Polkemmet's own generating plant, consisting of two Pearson turbo-alternators of 1,000 and 2,000 kilowatt capacity and one Metro-Vick machine producing a further 1,000 kilowatts providing an underground supply of 400 volts. The power supply was 120 watts, which was also the current supplied by the coal company to the miners' rows and one former miner recalls how when a coal cutter or any other machine was started up underground at Whitrigg, the lights in the miners' homes used to dim until they almost went out. Although the Whitburn pits had an underground electricity supply at the coal face the miners still needed the lamps on their helmets as is shown in this picture.

34 When they finished their work and came to the surface each miner was responsible for returning his lamp to the lamp cabin so that it could be fully charged ready for his next shift. In this photograph Richard McGregor is seen checking the lamps at Polkemmet. The lamps also provided an instant and important safety check of which miners were underground at any particular time.

35 The miners also carried Davy safety lamps like the one carried by Nisbet McPhail at Whitrigg Colliery. These lamps were designed to go out if there was any methane gas, which was also known as coal damp, thus giving the miners early warning of the likelihood of an explosion. Canaries were also kept underground in the pits as they were very sensitive to fire damp gas. The saying 'To fall of your perch', came from the fact that if the canary collapsed the miners knew they were in deadly danger and to escape immediately from the area. The miner standing next to Mr. McPhail is believed to be Davy Wilson. The names of their two companions are not known, but one of them appears to be enjoying a quick smoke, either before going underground or at the end of his shift, as cigarettes were strictly forbidden underground and taking matches down the shaft was an offence punishable by dismissal.

36   This photograph also shows Whitrigg Colliery miners, but what was the occasion for this smiling group picture? Whitrigg ceased production in 1972.

37 More of the men who worked at Whitrigg Colliery. Whitrigg was also known as The Lady, a nickname derived from Lady Baillie of Polkemmet House.

38 Although they spent their working lives in the darkness below ground, the miners at Whitrigg were reminded of the rural nature of their pit as soon as they came to the surface, as this picture with the farm hay stacks in the background is a reminder. As a result many of the miners' most popular pastimes were equally to do with the countryside, such as exercising their greyhounds and whippets and sometimes catching rabbits with them. As well as the illegal delights of occasional poaching, the miners also enjoyed the equally illicit thrills of betting on pitch and toss, a game of chance which depended on the fall of a coin and for which the haystacks often provided suitable cover from the eyes of the local police constabulary. The games of pitch and toss were usually played on Sunday afternoons and although lookouts were always posted a few of the miners were sometimes caught and were fined five shillings or as much as ten shillings for a repeat offence, at the burgh court on the following Monday morning.

39   More of the miners who
worked underground at
Whitrigg Colliery.

40 Miners at Whitrigg were enjoying their well-earned break when the photographer captured this picture in the years following the Second World War. Working at the coal face was dusty, dry, drouthy work and the miners often filled their metal bottles with cold sweetened tea, as they found this more refreshing than water. Their piece boxes were shaped with one end curved to accommodate the slices of bread with which their wives made their daily sandwiches. Popular fillings were Cheddar cheese and raspberry jam. It is often claimed that as a result of the seeds in the raspberry jam, there was often a rich crop of wild rasps to be picked on the surface above the mine workings.

41 These miners photographed at the coal face at Greenrigg Pit are Mr. Clark, who was the machine man and worked at the colliery for around thirty years, Wallace Swan, who was known as the second man, who worked behind the coal cutting machine shovelling the cuttings, and on the left Willie Paton, who was the shot firer. He is shown with his powder can of explosives. All three miners are wearing carbide lamps attached to their cloth caps and despite the dangers of their job have no safety clothing. Notice Mr. Paton's tackety boots. The coal cutting machine which they were operating is seen in the foreground.

42 These miners at Whitrigg Colliery included John Johnstone, George Middleton, Bill Bryce and George Waddell.

43 The opening of the first pithead baths at Polkemmet Colliery at the end of the 1920s was a very significant step forward in miners' welfare. No longer did the miners' wives have to boil gallons of water to fill the big tin baths, which they placed in front of the kitchen range, ready for their husbands to wash off the coal dust at the end of each shift. Now the miners could wash away the grime as soon as they reached the pithead. The two white coated attendants who were responsible for keeping the new bath house clean and tidy can be seen standing on the doorstep of the entrance as several of the miners, their wives, daughters and girl friends looked on after the opening ceremony.

44 Polkemmet was the last colliery in operation not just in Whitburn but the whole of West Lothian and was one of the most modern in Scotland with the latest coal cutting machinery as seen in this photograph taken underground at the coal face, when it was unfortunately very badly affected by the national miners' strike of the mid-1980s. Up until the strike its work force of 1,450 men were producing up to 2,250 tons of high quality coal for the Ravenscraig Steel Mill at Motherwell and with such a demand for its product its future seemed secure. During the prolonged time that it lay idle, however, flooding occurred and this together with the closure of its main customer, Ravenscraig, sealed its fate and the National Coal Board closed it in 1988. Its shut down was a devastating blow for Whitburn and it has taken the town a decade to start to recover.

45　Memories of happier times in Whitburn's coal mining industry are captured in this photograph of a Christmas party held in the Welfare Hall in the mid-1930s. The picture was taken by Mr. A. Bryce, who lived at 48 West Main Street. The red brick Welfare was the scene of much of Whitburn's social life from Saturday night dances to Burns Suppers. It was often referred to as the Big Hall. The Wee Hall, which was situated where the betting shop now stands on the opposite side of the street, was the town's picture house, where many Whitburn folk have fond memories of doing their courting while watching the latest black-and-white films of the 1930s and the new Technicolour ones of the 1940s. In the picture the clothes which the party guests wore provide many comments on the fashions of the period, from the hat worn by the lady on the right to the flat cap worn by the gentleman in the centre of the second back row.

46   In marked contrast to the ladies in their party finery in the previous picture, this one shows Whitburn women hard at work at the 'tattie havking' at Murraysgate Farm. The annual potato harvest was hard manual labour and boys and girls from the local schools were also allowed a week's leave of absence from the local schools each October, and the annual autumn mid-term week is still sometimes heard referred to as the tattie havking holidays.

47   Place names are a good way of discovering local history and Manse Road is a reminder of the church's connection with this part of Whitburn as it is named after the minister's home. This picture postcard view shows the scene looking to the north towards down the hill into the town centre. Another local place name the Glebe is also connected with local church history as it was originally the name given to the land granted to the minister so that he could grow his own vegetables and thus boost his annual stipend. Many place names in Whitburn come from the local farm which originally occupied the land such as Croftmalloch, which is thought to be derived from the Gaelic for the wee farm of rough ground, Murraysgate and Whitedalehead, meaning the upper part of the valley of the White Burn. Others such as Aitken Drive and Drysdale Avenue are named after former Provosts, while Baillie Street is named after the Baillie family who lived at Polkemmet House and White Street is called after Captain M. White, who left an inheritance in trust to help local poor people. Polkemmet is probably derived from Gaelic meaning the pool on the bend of the river Almond.

MANSE ROAD, WHITBURN

48   Historic Whitburn South Parish Church is a primly plain Presbyterian place of worship, whose only external adornment is its neat little stone bird cage belfry, from which the bell calls members of the Church of Scotland congregation to worship each Sunday. The other Church of Scotland congregation in the town meets at Brucefield. One of Whitburn's best known ministers was the Revd. William McMartin, who served Brucefield for forty-two years from 1935 to 1977. As well as faithfully serving his congregation, Mr. Martin was also chaplain to Tippethill Hospital and did much work for the West Lothian Scout Association and for the Sports Committee in Whitburn. Brucefield's new premises in East Main Street were built during Mr. Martin's ministry to cope with the increase in the congregation, attracted by his preaching and pastoral care.

49 In the graveyard at the South Parish Church lies buried the poet Robert Burn's illegitimate daughter, Elizabeth Paton. She was the wife of the overseer at Polkemmet Estate, John Bishop. Her mother, who was also called Elizabeth, was a servant in the Burns' household when the baby was born in 1785. The poet marked little Elizabeth's birth by writing a poem called 'Welcome'. In 1817, Elizabeth died young aged only thirty-two. Her husband and her daughter are also buried in the churchyard. There are many other interesting stones in the churchyard, dating from the 18th century, including the burial lair of the Baillie family, who lived at Polkemmet House.

50   As well as church choirs, Whitburn at one time had a choral union. It was founded towards the end of the First World War in 1917, when Mr. Sangster, who had previously been the choir master at Longridge, was persuaded to become its conductor. The choral union attracted over eighty members and they gave their first concert the following year. The twenty ladies and gentlemen of the choir seen in this photograph with their conductor and their accompanist, were chosen by a committee of members to represent Whitburn Choral Union in a county-wide competition open to all choirs in West Lothian. The Whitburn singers won the West Lothian Music Association Cup and the large silver rose bowl which they won is proudly displayed in the picture. Sadly, shortly after their triumph, Mr. Sangster decided to retire and the Choral Union was disbanded. Nowadays the town has its own amateur musical society which presents annual shows in the assembly hall of Whitburn Academy.

51 Whitburn Public School was the forerunner of the present Whitburn Academy and its classrooms are still used as an annex by the pupils of Whitdale Primary. Its stern grey stone architecture and grey slate roof was typical of the style of building of many Scottish schools, with its tall narrow classroom windows specifically designed to let light in, but to make it impossible for pupils to waste valuable lesson time by staring out of them. Anyone who did dare to day dream was liable to be brought sharply back to reality with a stinging, searing stroke of the strap. The two or three thonged thick leather tawse as it was officially described or 'the belt' as pupils nicknamed it, was administered to both boys and girls and was only abolished at the beginning of the 1980s. While Whitburn teachers were strict they were also very well respected and one of the most popular, Miss Margaret Allan, M.A. was granted the freedom of the Burgh in August 1967. Other Whitburn residents who have received this honour include Councillor David Drysdale and Mr. Robert Mickel.

52   School pupils of an earlier era watched inquisitively as the photographer set up his big camera and took this picture on a pleasant summer day in West Main Street. One of the early colour postcards which was produced from it, now in the collection of Mr. Douglas McIndoe, bears the postmark 1910. This interesting shot shows the style in which the children were dressed and how they could stand safely right in the centre of the street because of the complete absence of traffic.

53 In their sports uniform of white gym blouses and navy blue cotton gym pants, the girls of Whitburn Junior Secondary School netball team posed for the camera man with their coach, Miss Rankin, after winning the West Lothian Netball Association Championships against teams from Armadale, Bathgate, Linlithgow and Bo'ness amongst other places in the county in 1958. The girls in the back row are: Norma Potter, Jean Muirhead and Marion Denholm. Those in front are: Maureen Fox, Jean Robertson, Betty Denholm who was team captain, L. McLean and G. Harkin.

54 Whitburn Junior Secondary School also produced winning footballers as seen here as the boys of the school team posed with the cup, which they had won.

55   Coming more up to date in the early 1950s the Whitburn Junior Secondary footballers still turned out winning teams, including this one with young John Lambie holding the cup. The boys wore the school badge on their strip. Some of the boys are identified in the next caption.

56 Headmaster Mr. Willie Scott beamed proudly as he was photographed with the boys of his cup winning football team and their trainer, Robert Fordyce. The boys in the front row are: Lesley Brown, John Fordyce, John Lambie, ? Brodie and John Cook. First left in the back row is John Gardner and the third, fourth and fifth lads are George Brown, ? Williams and Wilson Wood.

57 Whitburn has always been famed for its interest in football. Most of the young miners played and this was the team which represented No.18 East Level in 1956. The line up was, back row: W. Traynor, E. Allan, W. Brown, W. Thomson, P. McInulty, T. Stewart and manager John Brown. Front: J. Hamilton, J. Bell, R. Campbell, who was team captain, T. Stewart and A. Haig.

58 That same year Under Manager Frank Matthews presented the medals at the end of the Douglas Cup Tournament. Here he is seen handing over medals to the runners-up in the final. The Douglas Cup was a competition run by Polkemmet Social Welfare Club. It was named after Mr. Douglas, a sub-contractor at the colliery, who presented the trophy. In its first year seven teams from various parts of the pit played for the new trophy, but subsequently interest waned and it was apparently never competed for again. Later West Lothian primary school football teams also competed fiercely on a knock out basis for a Douglas Cup, so perhaps this was what became of the trophy.

59 Best known of Whitburn's football teams is Whitburn Juniors seen here in action in the late 1950s. The player in the dark jersey is John Robertson, immediately behind him is goalkeeper Isaac Whiteford. On the right in the hooped shirt is Tom Stewart and Dick McGregor is seen in the background.

60 As well as being keen football players, Whitburn folk have also always been ardent football fans and here an enthusiastic group, complete with tartan tammies and scarves, are pictured on the pavement in front of the Baillie Institute waiting for the bus which was to take them south to London to see Scotland play England at Wembley Stadium in the mid-1950s. The big trip south took place every second year and many people saved regularly twenty-four months to be able to take part. Those in the back row of the picture are believed to include Willie Cornwell, Andrew Johnston, Peter Topping, Davy Liddle, Tina Topping, Babs Johnson, Jimmie Ronald, Johnnie Johnston and Willie Stirling. In the front row the supporters include Willie Johnston, John McNair, Bob Donald, Jamie Stevenson, Tommy Brodie, Owen McEwan and Jim Stevenson.

61 As well as travelling by bus, the people of Whitburn also used to be able to travel by train from the local station, which was situated at East Whitburn, where Mr. William Smellie was the last station master before it closed. By his time in the 1940s there were only goods trains, but previously there had been a passenger service. Here the station is seen when the railway was still a very popular means of travel. The station master with his gold watch on a chain, ready to check that the trains were on time, stands in front of the station name plate, while the posters on the wooden fence advertise Van Houten's Cocoa, a popular chocolate drink of the period and the poster on the brick wall of the ticket office and waiting room advertises shows an ocean liner and advertises voyages to Canada at a time when emigration offered local people the chance of a new life on the opposite side of the Atlantic. The house behind the station buildings belonged to the railway company and was the home of the station master and his family.

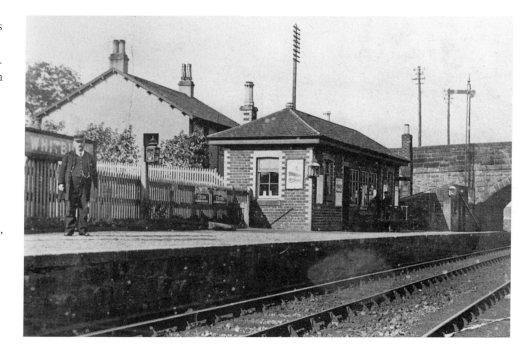

62   Near the railway station in East Whitburn the original old three-storey Goth Inn was a popular place to enjoy a refreshment. It acquired its unusual name from the Swedish city of Gothenburg, where the cooperative system of ownership of licensed premises, along similar lines to which the Whitburn pub was operated, was first established to try to encourage responsible drinking amongst the many sailors in the Scandinavian seaport. Other Gothenburgs in Scotland include the nearby local one in Armadale and one in Prestonpans. The Whitburn Goth's modern premises continue to be patronised by a loyal following.

63 Another social improvement which took place in Whitburn after the First World War was the building in the 1920s of the first of the new council houses. Built first at Murraysgate and then later at the Glebe, Jubilee Road, Union Road and other sites in the town by the local council, they were available at economic rents and with their indoor toilets and baths and their kitchens separate from the living rooms were a vast improvement on accommodation in the oldfashioned crowded miners' rows. One report described Whitburn's new council housing schemes as 'being laid out in garden city fashion with open spaces planted with flowers, parks and playing fields, which add colour and the interest of variety'.

New Houses, Whitburn

64   For the children who grew up in Whitburn in the 1920s and 1930s the annual Gala Day was one of the highlights of their young summers. The first Whitburn Gala was held in 1907. Four years later all the children who took part in the Gala Day in 1911 were presented with blue and white Dutch china mugs and little heart-shaped boxes of chocolates as souvenirs to commemorate the coronation of King George V and Queen Mary. This Gala photograph was taken some years later, probably around 1924, when the war memorial in the background had recently been erected in the newly-opened public park. The children in the picture may have been the successful competitors in a competition to make floral tributes to place at the memorial. Before the opening of the public park, the Gala Day crowning ceremony had taken place in fields belonging to various farmers including ones at the Glebe, Union Road and Jubilee Road as well as at Bog Park, on which Lomond Terrace was built.

65 The procession through the streets of the town has always been one of the highlights of Whitburn Gala and to this day it is one of the largest and most impressive of its kind in the whole country. A feature of Gala Days used to be the erection of impressive street-wide decorated arches, like the one seen in this picture postcard view. The first triple span arch was erected in 1913 at the East End and another impressive one was built the following year at the junction of Armadale Road and Lea Street. After the First World War the enthusiasm for the designing of arches covered in neatly clipped green box wood gathered from Polkemmet Estate and other parts of the countryside around the town reached its peak in the 1920s, when on one occasion four large arches decorated the procession route.

66 The schoolboy champion mounted on horse back is one of the best known sights of the Whitburn Gala Day parade. While the Queen's champion always had his pony to ride, other children had to walk and the length of the grand procession was one of the factors which led to East Whitburn establishing its own local Gala for its own children.

67 Isa Sangster, who later became Mrs. Brownlee, played the part of Britannia with her Union Jack shield and trident.

68 At the coronation ceremony at Whitburn Gala Day in 1947, Queen Helen Doolan was crowned by Mrs. D. Drysadale. In this photograph, taken shortly after she was crowned, Queen Helen was presented with her royal sceptre.

69 These imaginatively dressed entrants posed with their decorated bicycles in front of the school in 1911. The picture was taken by well-known Scottish postcard photographer Robert Braid from Livingston.

70 School pupils of a more modern age took part in this Gala Day parade which was photographed in the late 1950s or early 1960s. The day appears to have been chilly as the girls almost all wore coats over their new Gala Day dresses as they marched west past the Commercial Bank in West Main Street. The premises were later occupied by Fisher's bakery.

71 The sound of brass music is always a popular one on Gala Saturdays, especially when it is provided by the players of Whitburn Public Band. The band was founded in 1870 and this early photograph shows its players in 1898. The band was later named after its sponsors, the Murray International Metals Whitburn Brass Band and the David A. Hall Whitburn Band.

72 Whitburn Burgh Band is one of the finest in the country. Under its conductor Alex. Fleming from that other brass band stronghold, Bo'ness, it was in the top five in the Scottish Championship every year from 1968 to 1973 and was the national winner in 1968, 1970 and 1972. Under Mr. Fleming's successor, J. Harrison, Whitburn Burgh Band won the Scottish twice running in 1974 and 1975, a feat which it bettered in the 1980s when it was Scottish Champion four years in succession from 1980 to 1983 under the baton of Major P. Parkes. The band has played on many radio programmes including BBC Radio Two's famous 'Listen To The Band' and has also appeared on several television shows. The future of brass music in Whitburn seems safe, as several of Whitburn Academy's pupils play with the British Championship winning West Lothian Schools' Brass Band.

73 As well as making music Whitburn's residents have always shown their talents in many ways including taking part in amateur dramatics. The actors who took to the stage in this comedy presented in the Welfare Hall included in the back row, from left to right: Willie Fordyce, Alec Fordyce, Maffis Hamilton, Dave Drummond and Jim ?, with Bob Donald, Jimmy Stevenson and Sandy Bryce seated in the front row.

74 The residents of Lea Street turned out for this photograph, which ranged from the youngest baby to the oldest grannie. From the style of the clothes from the men's flat cloth caps to the little girl's school gym tunic the picture was probably taken in the late 1920s or early 1930s. Two of the men in the front row have placed their caps on their knees, which allows the full size of them to be seen. It was from their size that they received the nickname of 'doo'landers, meaning that they were broad enough for a pigeon to alight upon.

75 This picture of another group of Whitburn residents was more formally posed by the photographer, with the children seated at the front and most of their smartly-suited fathers standing in a row at the back. The identity of the couple in the centre and what they were celebrating is, however, lost in the mists of history. The white-bearded gentleman seated at the end of the second row may be the same one who appears in an earlier picture taken at the Cross.

76 Well 'happit' against the winter cold, Mrs. Janet Thomson was photographed seated in front of the glowing fire of her kitchen range, with her pet dog also clearly enjoying the warmth tucked in neatly at her feet. The kettle is simmering away on top of the range, ready to infuse a nice cup of tea. On the back of the chair there is a patch work rug, which Mrs. Thomson may well have knitted.

From age to youth this Whitburn laddie, also had his dog with him when the photographer took this picture of him sitting on the Eppistane on the outskirts of the town. The stone takes its name from the local woman found guilty of witchcraft and executed here. Despite its grim history it has long been a popular summer play place for Whitburn children.